PIANO / VOCAL / GUITAR

# Gary Barlow Since I Saw You Last

WISE PUBLICATIONS
*part of The Music Sales Group*
London / New York / Paris / Sydney / Copenhagen / Berlin / Madrid / Hong Kong / Tokyo

Published by
*Wise Publications*
14-15 Berners Street, London W1T 3LJ, UK.

Exclusive Distributors:
*Music Sales Limited*
Distribution Centre, Newmarket Road,
Bury St Edmunds, Suffolk IP33 3YB, UK.
*Music Sales Pty Limited*
Units 3-4, 17 Willfox Street, Condell Park,
NSW 2200, Australia.

Order No. AM1008733
ISBN: 978-1-78305-514-2
This book © Copyright 2014 Wise Publications,
a division of Music Sales Limited.

Edited by Jenni Norey.
Music arranged by Alistair Watson.
Music processed by Paul Ewers Music Design.
Original sleeve design and art direction: Studio Fury.
Cover photograph by Phil Poynter.

Printed in the EU.

# Requiem

Words & Music by Robbie Williams & Gary Barlow

Thy will___ was done,___ oh wipe that wor - ry from___
no one___ fa - mous.___ Please don't pa - nic, it

___ your face.___ You'll die when you___ see my___ new place___ but
looks so tra - gic, all switch - ing seats___ on the___ Ti - ta - nic. I'm

do the time___ you're in for___ life.___ Oh my
sad to go___ hope you en - joy the___ show.___ Oh my

(%) friends I hear you sing,___ The Lord's___ My Shep - herd real - ly, what a song to sing.___
friends I hear you say,___ a lot of love - ly things a - bout me here to - day.___

6

in Re - qui - em,___ with all my___ friends,___

with all my___ friends,___

with all my___ friends,___

with all my___ friends.___

9

# Let Me Go

Words & Music by Gary Barlow

1. A room full of sadness, a bro - ken heart. And on - ly me to blame for ev - 'ry sin - gle part.

loved. So this is gon-na take_ a bit of get-ting used_ to, but I know what's

right for you.     Fly

high_____ and let me go.     That

sky_____ will save your soul.

high_____ and let me go.          That

sky_____ will save your soul.          When you pass_

by,_____ then you'll know          that

this is gon-na take_ a bit of get-ting used_ to, but I know what's right for you.          So

15

# Jump

Words & Music by Gary Barlow & Tim Rice Oxley

jump, high. If you want a bet-ter view, then an-oth-er life is call-ing you to go a-head and try___ now___ or how you gon-na find___ out.___ If life has got pre-dic-ta-ble, go on do some-thing won-der-ful. The first step is the hard-est, you'll be safe with-out a har-ness so jump, jump. 2. You

*To Coda*

1.

# Face To Face

Words & Music by Gary Barlow & John Shanks

true sign___ of a sol - dier
(2.) mea-sure the strength of a hu - man

tak - ing care of the hearts___ a - round___
by the weight of the love___ a - round___

___ us.___ And the whole world___ loves a he - ro, a
___ them.___ One sweet light___ in the dark - ness,

lead - er and a shoul - der to cry___ on,___ that's what you are___ to me,___
guid - ed us all___ like a pi - lot, that's what you are___ to me,___

___ ev - 'ry - one a - round___ can see,___ yeah. When we're face___
___ ev - 'ry - one a - round___ be - lieves,___ yeah.

# God

Words & Music by Gary Barlow

1. Per - se - vere, keep on search - ing, they
2. Try your faith and all their ans - wers

gua - ran - tee that one day we'll be found.
all been quot - ed from the book of man.

Could an-y-one real-ly be that cruel?____ To keep the

king of heav-en and___ earth___ right next to you.____

*D.S. al Coda*

They

Ⓒ *Coda*

____ If you found___ God,___ if you found God___ would it

32

# Small Town Girls

Words & Music by Gary Barlow

# 6th Avenue

*Words & Music by Gary Barlow & John Shanks*

# We Like To Love

Words & Music by Gary Barlow

1. Stand-ing here with-out__ you I've got noth-ing to say, seems my guar-dian an-gel had the

# Since I Saw You Last

Words & Music by Gary Barlow

1. They

took my voice,____ e - ras - ed my past,____ with

all that noise___ it could-n't last.___ With
words so cruel___ I washed my face,___ I
hoped one day___ I'd wake up in a bet-ter place.___ To-
-day I took___ back what___ was sto-len and gave new life___ to what___

54

since I saw___ you last._____

2. When bro-thers land___ and

3. I know you heard___ my

take what's good,___ you can win a war___

shout for help,___ for those who stood___ and___ watched___

**1.**

oh,___ and shed no blood.___ Ev-'ry-bod-y

go

56

# This House

Words & Music by Gary Barlow & John Shanks

O-pen the doors and win - dows, whole world in - side these four walls,

more than a build - ing, floor to the ceil - ing, a pic - ture of love.

*To Coda*

That's this house.

# Dying Inside

Words & Music by Gary Barlow

soon. No-bod-y knows what I'm go-ing through. I'm

dy - - ing in - side. Who knows what I'm think-ing, what I'm

try - ing to hide. Yeah, I'm dy - - ing all night. I'm

breath-ing but I can't feel life, I'm smil-ing but I'm dy'n' in -

# More Than Life

*Words & Music by Gary Barlow*

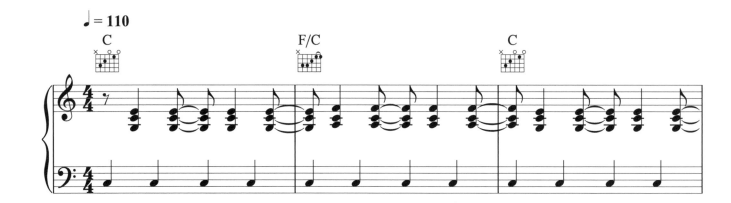

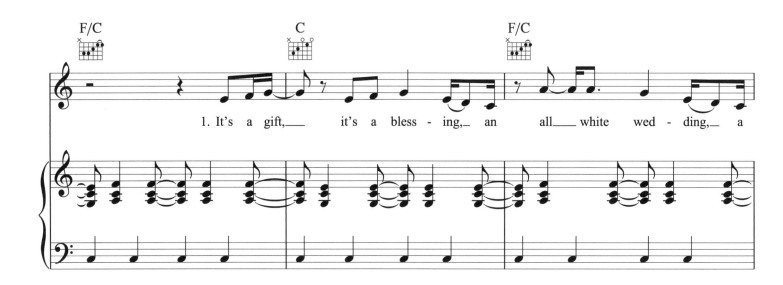

1. It's a gift,___ it's a bless - ing,___ an all___ white wed - ding, a

peace - ful morn - ing___ in June. It's a crown,___ it's a call - ing, a

your child's first birth-day, now get some sleep. It's that feel-ing in your heart, it's one

drink too far, it's a brand new car, you can drive your-self. It's when

vi-si-tors have gone, it's your fa-v'rite song, it's a sing-a-long so let's

sing a-long. This love's got stron-ger with time and this

123456789

# Bringing you the words and the music

All the latest music in print... rock & pop plus jazz, blues, country, classical and the best in West End show scores.

- Books to match your favourite CDs.
- Book-and-CD titles with high quality backing tracks for you to play along to. Now you can play guitar or piano with your favourite artist... or simply sing along!
- Audition songbooks with CD backing tracks for both male and female singers for all those with stars in their eyes.
- Can't read music? No problem, you can still play all the hits with our wide range of chord songbooks.
- Check out our range of instrumental tutorial titles, taking you from novice to expert in no time at all!
- Musical show scores include *The Phantom Of The Opera*, *Les Misérables*, *Mamma Mia* and many more hit productions.
- DVD master classes featuring the techniques of top artists.

Visit your local music shop or, in case of difficulty, contact the Marketing Department, Music Sales Limited, Newmarket Road, Bury St Edmunds, Suffolk, IP33 3YB, UK
marketing@musicsales.co.uk